A special thanks to Dr. John
Telford, a friend and mentor

Without his support and encouragement this work
of poems would never have been written or
published.

I0161552

LIST OF POEMS

VIKING RIGHT OF PASSAGE

BALDR'S QUEST FOR A BRIDE

KING RAGNAR'S EXECUTION

THE THEFT OF SWENSEN'S BEARD

THE RITUAL

DANCE OF THE MAIDENS

THE DRAKKAR

THE EXECUTION

THE VIKING MAIDEN

THE OLD MAN

THE STORM

THE TRAPPER'S DOGS

THE RAID

THE HOMECOMING

THE TALLASMAN

THE BESERKER

THOR

ODIN'S PROMICE

KING RAGNAR'S REVENGE

DONALD FREDERICKSON

A VIKING'S
RIGHT OF PASSAGE

I.

The wind blew strong and the chill was biting.
The little fire held the cold at bay.
The bent old man hunched to embrace the hearth,
His thoughts on an earlier day.
Twas of his youth his mind returned,
To a spring in the month of May.

The bow cut the waves with the force of an ax;
The wind it strongly blew.
The sails were filled with Oden's breath,
And the spray bit cold and true.
The long boat braced by the White Oak's strength
Southward swiftly flew.

A dragon's-head prow led the warrior's quest;
Its eyes, they seemed to glow.
"On to the land of the Celts," it said,
Their future it seemed to know.
"It's spring! It's spring!" the dragon cried,
"And southward we must go."

TALES OF THE VIKINGS

In Thor's great name he'd hold his own
With battle ax and shield.
His muscles strong, his manner bold,
His pride as a warrior revealed.
The coming battle would be his first,
And he'd be upon the field.

Southward they sailed to the land of the Celts
Where plunder and riches are found.
The warriors of Oden would risk their lives,
To their code of honor bound.
To kill or die it mattered not,
But to have fought well is renowned.

Soon they'd find a Celtic town,
And he would face the test,
To show he had a warrior's heart,
And courage, like all the rest.
He would fight with his great strength,
To which, all would attest.

The warrior's code was Oden's given,
But a man's good name his own.
It's the deeds in life that he has done
That really will be shown.
When he leaves this world it's all that stays,
It's how he's always known.

Life is hard in the Norsemen's world
The warriors among the best,

But honor, courage, and a man's good name
Must always pass the test.
The time draws near for the warrior's rite,
And he'd pass just like the rest.

The young man's dream of wealth and fame
Held down his gnawing fear.
He'd signed to sail a longboat quest
And his test came steadily near.
The wind blew hard and the waves were high,
As he tightly gripped his spear.

The boat sailed south and the dragon laughed,
And a pact with hell was made.
The young man came to a grim resolve
To meet death by the blade.
A better death no man could find,
His debt to Oden paid.

And the boat sailed south to the land of the
Celts
Where the Viking name was feared.
Their skills with sword, and ax and spear
Were grudgingly revered.
And the dragon laughed at the smell of blood,
As southward it strongly peered.

II.

The old man placed a log on the fire
For its warmth he seemed to yearn.
He felt the warmth of his first test passed
As he watched the fire burn.
And with a smile upon his face,
To his youth he did return.

The blood flowed fast and red that day.
The Vikings took their toll.
The Celts stood firm to save their homes,
Upon the grassy knoll.
But Norsemen fight with the fury of hell,
For Oden owns their soul.

His ax swung hard and met it's mark.
His shield did brace the blow.
For battle he'd been trained since youth,
The warrior's way he'd show.
With strength, and speed, and ferocity,
His name they'd come to know.

A head bashed here, an arm slashed there,
His ax ripped through a chest.
Much Celtic blood was spilled that day,
He'd surely passed the test.

DONALD FREDERICKSON

The Celts fell short and died and died.
They'd tangled with the best.

His test of manhood came that day,
The Ax did mark the score.
Blood lust rose within his head,
And he wanted more and more.
He'd done the deeds that warriors do
As he battled up that shore.

Foes he slew and the wounds he took,
As power rushed to his head.
Invincible he'd thus become, a warrior of the clan,
A Viking chief he'd be one day to fill the world with dread.
And on and on, he slew his foes.
And, the blood flowed strong and red.

The dragon watched from his place on shore
As they burnt and sacked the land.
It was spring again and the rite of blood
Was sought by the raiding band.
To the land of the Celts they came once more
To rob and kill as planned.

The greatest gain was a warrior's name,
With the deeds that he had done.

TALES OF THE VIKINGS

The young man entered their world that day.
With the victories he had won.
For a Viking warrior is known and feared
His superior there is none.

III.

The old man dwelled on that day long past
As the fire became an ember.
A warrior he was made that day,
And his deeds they'd long remember,
As they sang their songs to recount their praise
On cold nights in December.

A warrior's life he had lived with pride,
It lasted many years.
His word was truth, his deeds were bold--
A man among his peers.
On Oden's face he'd one day look.
The time was drawing near.

The fire died out and the cold crept in,
But the old man didn't know.
The long boat came with the dragon prow,
And the shields all in a row.
The dragon laughed as his eyes glowed red
And he said, "It's time to go!"

DONALD FREDERICKSON

The bows cut the waves with the force of an ax,
The wind, it strongly blew
The sails were filled with Oden's breath,
And the spray was cold and true.
The boat was filled with the old man's deeds,
To its course it quickly flew.

Off to the land of the underworld,
The land far down below.
Off to the land of the underworld,
To the land all warriors go.
Off to the land of the underworld,
Where your name they'll sure to know.

BALDR'S QUEST FOR A BRIDE

New fallen snow, caressed by the moon's cold
blue light,
Blankets the world, through the winter's long
night.
Frozen white waves, shaped by the wind from
the north;
A sea of ice ridges, where no boat goes forth.
A scene of great beauty, this cold desolate
place,
In the light of the moon, a smile from its face.

The crunch of the snow, beneath shodded feet,
Played softly the sound, of a cold lonely beat.
His horse picked a path o'er the iced covered
lane,
A trail through the trees that lead to the plain.
A path to be traveled. It lead him as planned
To the mead hall of Ragnar, the King of Jutland.

He'd claim for his own the daughter of kings,
Or meet his death trying, whichever fate brings.

Young men before tried using their might,
Stood up to the Gorkin, and put up a fight.
Sealing their fate without due recourse,
Each was dispatched, with deadly force.

The young man gazed at the face of the moon,
Envisioning the smile the maid in full bloom.
Her hair was bright gold, in the morning sun-
light,
And shining blue eyes sparkled into the night.
Loved her he did, from the moment they met,
Have her he must; his determination set.

Down from the North he rode a great horse
The son of a Viking, a man of great force.
His courage before him, the source of his pride,
He'd fight the wild Gorkin, to win his fair bride.
The beautiful Erika, the love of his life,
With the blessing of Oden would soon be his
wife.

He sought the great hall all covered in snow,
Set by the shore, where swift waters flow.
The lair of the King Ragnar, the lord of the sea;
Ruler of two kingdoms , a fate his to be.
Danesland and Sweden each land of the Norse,
He joined together with vengeance and force.

TALES OF THE VIKINGS

The hall of the king is the place for his throne,
And the warriors of Oden consider it home.
On long winter nights when the sea is all ice,
The men of the clan will drink and play dice.
They'll sing and tell stories of conquests long
past,
Recounting brave deeds, from memories that
last.

A place of great merriment, a place for a fight,
The Hall of the Vikings came alive every night.
With drinking and laughter there came a great
roar,
From men of the north, bound by ice to the
shore.
To drown out the silence of long winter nights,
And wait for the spring, for raids and for fights.

The young man could see, when the hall came
in sight,
A light bright and sharp, which pierced the cold
night.
He paused for a moment to survey the land,
Here he had come and here he would stand.
His fate stood before him, which way would it
go,
To the warmth of the mead hall, or a cold grave
below?

DONALD FREDERICKSON

§

The Gorkin was chained from ankle to floor,
A beast of eight feet and a few inches more.
Dirty and grungy, he sits with his shame,
A captive of Vikings who knew not his name.
They sat out of range and threw him some scraps,
And laughed at the beast, caught in one of their traps.

Five hardy men had brought the beast down.
A Gorkin is vicious, for which he's renown.
The killer of men, which he hunts in the night,
A creature all fear, who puts them to flight.
Now chained to the floor of Ragnar's great hall,
He waits his next victim, a man he can maul.

His anger is rage; he'll kill anyone near.
His captors torment him, as something to fear.
He braves every onslaught, providing fierce roars,
That resound through the hall and rattle the doors.
T'is a beast of great courage, one few men have met,
In Ragnar's great hall, he's the king's favorite pet.

§

He threw open the doors and rode in on his
horse,
As ice coated air flowed o'er the men of the
Norse.
All eyes turned toward him; not one word was
said.
They knew of his quest, but soon he'd be dead.
Another man comes to seek Erika's hand.
Another they'd bury, in this cold frozen land.

"I've come for my true love," he shouted to all,
As he sat on his horse and scanned the great
hall.
"Erica my love, " he called into the night,
"I am Lord Baldr, for your love I will fight."
"I'll kill the wild Gorkin and take you from here,
His death will come quickly, there's nothing to
fear."

The Gorkin looked up, as a smile crossed his
face.
Another he'd kill in this horrible place.
He'd rip off an arm, as they watched in cold
fear,
To eat raw and bloody, since none would come
near.
He'd eat good tonight, the flesh of this man
Who came here to fight, and would die by his
hand.

DONALD FREDERICKSON

Erika beamed as the young man came forth,
Baldr, first son of a chief from the north.
Bold was his manner, the mark of a man.
He came from his kingdom to fight for her hand.
Joy flooded her being. her heart opened wide.
He came here to fetch her; It filled her with
pride.

Then to the Gorkin, her eyes moved unbid;
And saw on his face, a smile hardly hid.
Suitors before, he'd killed with dispatch.
Would Baldr her love, be up for the match?
A husband she wanted, and not daddy's pet.
Death to the Gorkin, his fate must be met.

Ragnar the king, yelled with all of his might,
"Ah, there young Baldr, you've come for the
fight.
See my fair daughter, your prize if you win.
Her maidenhood's pure, with a man she's not
been.
The love in your eyes, glows strong in my sight,
Defeat the wild Gorkin, and she's yours to-
night."

The young man slowly got down from his horse.
With his sword and ax he would manage the
course.

TALES OF THE VIKINGS

He eyed his opponent, a frown crossed his face;
Many before him had been in his place.
He turned back to Erika, love burning so strong,
"Don't worry my love. This won't take me
long."

The Gorkin reached out and grasped his club
tight.
He'd use it to kill this young man tonight.
The club was well known for the danger it held,
Twenty had challenged and twenty it felled.
Large as a man and studded with spikes,
The weapon was deadly, killing quickly in the
fights.

The beast stood and watched, a scowl on its
face,
And stared at the man who would die in this
place.
The men formed a circle, the bounds of the
fight,
The arena of battle, on such a cold night.
A fight to the death is sport in this land.
And with a great roar, they cheered the young
man.

Boldly he entered the circle of men,
His arms were raised high, for the fight to begin.

DONALD FREDERICKSON

His ax in his left hand, his sword in his right,
His opponent a Gorkin, a beast of the night.
The beast stood there waiting, hate shown from
its face,
To kill with no feeling, not even a trace.

A large muscled body and eight feet in height,
A killer of men, is dangerous to fight,
The club in his large hand, its wrath he would
bring.
His body was tense and ready to spring.
He pulled his head back and emitted a roar,
And with a great swing the club flew toward the
floor.

The blow missed its mark as the lord jumped
away,
Rolling off to the side like a young boy at play.
He rose to full height and held his sword high,
And shouted out loudly, "It's time that you die."
He stood there defiant, facing his foe,
And down came the club, with another great
blow.

His sword and ax met the strong vicious charge,
Trading blow upon blow with this beast, oh so
large.

The Gorkin, raging in anger at the pace of the
fight,
His club held with both hands, swung with all of
his might.
Striking the sword, like a twig in the breeze,
Knocking the young lord down to his knees.

Blows from above, with his back to the floor,
The lord from the north felt the malice they
bore.
Blow after blow he'd fend off or dodge,
The crash of the club rang throughout the
lodge.
The Gorkin grew furious, his rage uncontrolled;
He screamed in frustration, his aggression more
bold.

§

The daughter of Ragnar, looked on with a fright.
Strong was her fear, as she watched Baldr's
plight.
She mouthed a small prayer. from her heart it
came forth,
Pleading for victory, from the gods of the north.
"Of him I've dreamed, in the dark of night.
Please give him strength to continue this fight."

DONALD FREDERICKSON

The gods of the Norsemen, looked down from
above,
Hearing the prayer of this maiden in love.
The handsome young noble, a lord from the
north,
Bleeding and broken, and still he came forth.
Love carried him onward, to fight without rest,
Though skilled as a warrior, he'd not pass the
test.

Oden looked down from his throne in the sky.
A smile crossed his face, as he let out a sigh.
The young lord could quit, for it was quite plain,
He had only to back past the Gorkin's stout
chain.
But quit he would not, and with honor he'd die.
For the love of the maiden, he still had to try.

§

The Gorkin was furious, the man's still alive.
How in the world could this one to survive?
He swung a strong blow, one of his best,
And caught the young lord, full in the chest,
Who tumbled and skidded and finally lay still.
The Gorkin roared loudly, t'was time for the kill.

He swung his great club with all of his might,
Down at young Baldr to finish the fight.
The aim of the blow was missed by a hair.
The young Viking warrior no longer was there.
Swinging his ax, Baldr struck a hard blow,
Which caught the wild Gorkin, and cut off his
toe.

The scream of the beast, split the air of the
night,
As rage rose within him, from this turn of the
fight.
He stopped for a moment, the pain was intense.
Another blow followed beneath his defense.
And into his foot, the ax struck again.
Here was a weakness, he could not defend.

The Gorkin swung wildly, without rhyme or
plan.
Baldr now faced him on foot like a man.
His sword slashed the arm, the one with the
club,
Cutting it off, leaving only a stub.
He whirled in a circle, his sword held out
straight,
Catching the neck and sealing its fate.

DONALD FREDERICKSON

The head rolled toward Ragnar, and stopped at
his feet.
It ended the fight with the Gorkin's defeat.
Baldr still shaking said "I claim my bride.
She'll come to my kingdom and reign by my
side."
And looking toward Erika, "You're mine now,"
he said.
"We'll finish this night in our wedding bed."

Two horses together, walked side by side,
Into the snow covered world they would ride.
The icy blue moon looked down from above,
A smile on its face for the two so in love.
Baldr and Erika rode out of that land.
The quest for his bride, went exactly as
planned.

King Ragnar's Execution

Day and night, for weeks on end, he searched
upon the sea,
 Along the coast of their fine land, to set his
people free.
Ella, King of England, was tired of his plight,
He'd rid the world of Vikings, and cast them
from his sight.
To all, he vowed to end this scourge, the raiders
from the north
With justice and a mighty hand, that was his to
bring forth.

He sought the Viking raider, Ragnar their King,
And, with righteous indignation, a vengeance
he would bring.
Upon the man who came each year, with his
raiding band,
And cast a reign of terror that ran throughout
the land.
They'd kill and maim his subjects, and take what
ere they please,

Then flee onto the cold dark sea, upon a way-
ward breeze.

With his great armada, he sailed the Eastern
coast,
Searching for an adversary who was just like a
ghost.
Upon the seas he could not catch, the Viking
king that was his quest.
The longboats of the Vikings, were obviously
the best,
When pulled with oars in water, that was not
very deep,
Or sailing o're the great cold sea, which was
within their keep.

He set a trap for those he sought, and carefully
he planned,
To catch them on a coastal raid, when they
were on dry land.
He'd have his soldiers waiting, within a stand of
wood,
Beside a peaceful village, where a little chapel
stood.
Upon a Christian feast day, he knew they'd
make a raid.
A day of Viking preference, t'is how their game
is played.

TALES OF THE VIKINGS

The sound of voices singing, drifts up into the
skies,
Along with joyous laughter, across the water
flies.
The people dance to sounds of flutes, in wild
abandonment,
Upon the churche's holy grounds, in joy and
merriment.
They celebrate a holiday, to hold their god in
praise
Who keeps them safe within his fold, through-
out these trying days.

From his mighty war ship the, king looked
across the sea
A town was there with riches that soon were his
to be.
He set a course that headed west, and to the
sandy shore,
To make a raid upon the town, which surely
they'd deplore.
It is his right to raid and loot, and plunder when
he could.
Within the code of his cruel world, he acted as
he should.

Upon the beach the sailing ships were ground-
ed on the sand,
And from them poured the warriors, who rav-
ished o're the land.

DONALD FREDERICKSON

They charged the celebration, and those before
them fled,
Away from Viking warriors, who held the world
in dread.
The village square now empty, held only Rag-
nar's men,
Who laughed at those ran away, their town
they'd not defend.

A battle cry soon cut the air; it came from in the
wood,
Followed by the charging men; the plan had
started good.
Ella, King of England, his trap a great surprise,
His soldiers hit the Vikings hard, before they'd
realize,
That Ragnar, King of Danesland, was in his
mighty grip,
And it was clutched around him tight, from
which he could not slip.

"Within my grasp, I have you now, and you'll
not get away,"
The English king told Ragnar, upon this fateful
day.
"No longer will you sack my land and take what
e're you please.
Today was your last day to raid. I've brought
you to your knees."

And to my dungeon you will go to wait for your
demise.
There'll be no honor in your death, by methods
I'll devise.

Into a pit of viperous snakes, they cast the Vi-
king chief,
To die a slow and painful death, to which was
their belief.
Would bring dishonor on his soul, and to the
gods implore,
To Keep him from an afterlife, a fate that he'd
deplore.
They watched in fascination, a man who
wouldn't bend,
And as he fought the venomous snakes, he
cursed them to the end.

Behind him Ragnar left three sons, their father
they did hate.
They tried to steal his kingdom once, banish-
ment was their fate.
They too were Viking raiders, along the Scottish
shore,
Who felt a need for vengeance, for this act they
did deplore.
And with the news of Ragnar's death they con-
sidered it their right,
To westward sail to England's coast, and there
put up a fight.

DONALD FREDERICKSON

The English army met them square, resisting
the attack,
And after a great battle, to Denmark sent them
back.
The oldest son of Ragnar, in England he would
stay
And with conniving methods, put another plan
in play
He called upon his brothers to come again and
fight.
T'was time to take their vengeance. It was their
Viking right.

The battle was a victory in which the Vikings
won
And then the rule of England, went to Ragnar's
oldest son.
His first act as a ruler, in which he did proclaim,
To have his Nordic vengeance, and restore his
father's name.
Death for a death was his command, for honor
it would bring,
And to the hangman's rope he sent, the now
defeated king.

This is the tale of Ragnar, the mighty Viking
chief
Who's death they truly thought, would give
them some relief.

TALES OF THE VIKINGS

To kill him without honor, and proper dignity,
Offended his three wayward sons, and their
integrity.
And in the aftermath, of the vengeance they
had planned
The Viking Sons of Ragnar, now ruled o're all
the land.

DONALD FREDERICKSON

The Theft of Swensen's Beard

On winter nights when cold creeps in, and ice is
on the shore,
The Drakkars bound in frigid clutch, will sail
again no more.
The Viking men of Ragnar's hoard will feast and
sing a song,
About the raids on England's coast, of summer
now long gone,
To tell the tales of warriors' might, when wheel-
ing ax or sword,
And bring home all the spoils or war, which
were their just reward.

Platters filled with beef and fowl, to quell their
appetites,
Are served by pretty maidens, upon such festive
nights.
Their liquor made of honey, a highly potent
brew,

31

Ran freely from the jug to lips and soon before
they knew,
Their tongues were loose for singing, about last
summer's quest.
And rough and battled warriors sang, each pro-
claiming to be best.

Their boasts lay claim to daring feats upon the
battle field,
Of how they fought in Oden's name; their brav-
ery revealed.
One by one, they took their place to raise a mug
in toast,
And tell the story of their feats with a strong
and mighty boast.
Each man sought to claim his place, and boast
about his valor,
While others laughed with snide remarks to,
make the speaker pallor.

Upon the table climbed a man, with sword and
battered shield,
To tell, to those who drank with him, about the
battle field.
His voice boomed with a resonance, about the
feats incurred,
And how he fought with Thor's great strength;
and all the while he slurred.
A mighty warrior self proclaimed, upon this
recent quest,

He fought with skill and bravery, to be the very
best.

He told a tale of armor shed, and naked to the
waist,
He charged the Celts defensive line, to be the
first they faced.
They called him a berserker, a daft and crazy
fool,
Who, when the rage consumed him, just let the
anger rule.
And with no fear of dying, he crashed into the
line,
A symbol of the Viking horde, a feared and
hated sign.

Upon the table's other end, up climbed another
man
Who said," Swensen you damn fool, t'was not
the battle plan.
Advance we would, but slowly, and make them
want to flee
In fear of our great wrath, and the battle that
would be.
We then would take what e're we would, with-
out a vicious fight
And put their gold within our ships, with just a
show of might."

Swensen slapped his sword against his shield,
and belched with all his might.
"A damn poor Viking you've become, I didn't
see you fight.

I went to fight; that's what I do, when we go on
a raid."
He wavered on uncertain feet, and swung his
iron blade.
"You stood behind and watched me, and little
else you did.
And when it came to fighting, I think you really
hid."

His words were thick and slurred, as the liquor
took its toll,
And Swensen stared through blurry eyes and he
knew he'd lost control.
His friend he'd have to fight now, and likely take
his life.
The words he could not take back, and then he
saw the knife.
Atop the table both men stood, and glared with
great intent,
As liquor held them in its bounds, each could
not relent.

"I'll kill you for your lying words," Hathgar
stoutly said,
"And when we place you in the ground, the
demons will be fed."

And in the fog, the drink bestowed, he laughed
without control
At thoughts of the harsh punishment, to which
he would extol
Upon the vicious warrior, who laughed along
with him.
He'd use the knife within his grip and kill with-
out a whim.

Swensen took a step and stumbled, and off the
table fell.
Upon the floor he dumbfound sat, within the
liquor's spell.
He rose to rings of laughter from those who
were around,
And stumbled forth unsure of foot, until a drink
he found.
He downed a jug filled to the brim and mellow
he became.
The liquor was the winner, and made the war-
rior tame.

From the table Hathgar jumped, revenge upon
his mind.
Another jug or two he'd drink, then Swensen he
would find.
"Where are you going Viking?" he called into
the night.
"It's time to pay for your cruel words; it's time
to stand and fight."

He stumbled as he walked, and slurred as he
proclaimed
He'd kill the other on this night, for honor he
defamed.

Upon the floor sat Swensen, his back against a
door,
And in his hand another jug, in case he wanted
more.
And in a drunken stupor, he finally had passed
out,
No longer with a care at all; not for the coming
bout.
A smile there was upon his face, a look that was
content.
The liquor held him in its grip, to which it'd not
relent.

Hathgar walked unsure of foot, to do the deadly
deed.
In one hand he clutched a knife; in the other a
jug of mead.
And there upon the floor, his blurry eyes did
see,
The old berserker now asleep, who could no
longer flee.
He stared at Swensen's long red beard, his
source of manly pride;
The symbol of the Viking hoard from which the
world did hide.

DONALD FREDERICKSON

From ear to ear the hair did flow, a bright and
shinning red;
a sign known to his enemies that filled their
hearts with dread.
The man that they called Swensen, was known
throughout the land
As the Viking with the long red beard, who'd
always take a stand,
And fight with any to the death, when honor
was at stake.
Behind him lay a trail of blood that followed in
his wake.

Within his drunken fog filled mind, Hathgar
formed a plan
To take from this old warrior, his right to be a
man.
Another jug of liquor downed, and time to con-
template,
Hathgar giggled to himself; he now knew Sw-
ensen's fate.
The beard he grasp within his hand, and slashed
it with his knife.
Thus he'd have his just revenge, and Swensen
still his life.

He held the beard for all to see the wicked deed
he'd done,
And laughed with all the other men who
thought it gleeful fun.

Another jug of honey brew, he downed with
joyful zest,
And next to Swensen he sat down; he'd take a
needed rest .
Against the wall he braced his back, his legs he
did extend,
And soon was snoring long and loud, along with
his old friend.

§

The morning chill was cold and damp, and
pierced down to the bone,
And peaking o're the fiord's great hills, the sun
now finally shown.
The two old warriors slowly woke, pain driving
through their heads,
And shivered at the thought, they'd not slept in
warm beds.
The liquor they'd consumed, no longer made
them warm.
And, sick they were from its effect, became the
morning norm.

Hathgar grasp his head with shaking hands, and
stared through blurry eyes.
He tried to focus on his friend, and then he real-
ized
The great flamboyant red beard, this Viking's
source of pride,

DONALD FREDERICKSON

The symbol of his mighty strength, on which
Swensen relied,
No longer was upon his chin, but on the ground
did lay--
A tangled clump of bright red hair; how did it
get that way?

He struggled to remember; then wanted to
forget
This act of wanton vengeance, the one he did
commit.
He looked upon the bright red hair that lay
upon the ground,
And knew that soon a good excuse was needed
to be found.
For Swensen was a vengeful man, as deadly as
they come;
But as far as smartness goes, he was considered
dumb.

Hathgar squinted hard, and peered through
bloodshot eyes.
If his next words were not correct, it may be his
demise.
"What happened to your great red beard? You
lost it in the night.
There was a great commotion and a shinning
source of light.
And in its sphere was mighty Thor, the warrior
god of thunder.

T'was standing in its radiant glow in all his
splendid wonder."

"A sword he held in one hand, in the other was
your beard.
There was a smile upon his face, a grin to be
revered.
Within the locks of your red beard, there is a
source of might;
A power reserved for gods alone, which is their
precious right.
Thor was jealous of your great beard; he has
none of his own,
And he considered you a threat, to sit by Oden's
throne."

Hathgar stared at Swensen's face, to gage his
word's effect.
He had to spin a tale of lies, that would his life
protect.
For Swensen had a temper, and if he even
thought
That his friend was lying, his life would be for
naught.
"The power in your great red beard, Thor stole
within the night,
For you he holds in morbid fear, that soon he'd
have to fight."

"With your beard upon your face, a god you'd
surly be,

DONALD FREDERICKSON

And rise up to the heavens for everyone to see.
Then as a mighty warrior, you'd fight the god
named Thor,
In Oden's kingdom high above, it's what you'd
have in store.
You'd leave the God of Thunder defeated by
your hand,
And you'd be praised by all the gods within
their sacred land."

From his eye, a tear rolled down and dropped
onto the hair,
And Swensen blankly stared at it, while
wrapped in his despair.
"A Viking warrior that I be, a man of girt and
might.
And, with the strength my red beard, I'd gladly
stand and fight.
I'd surly kill the mighty Thor, and take his place
on high.
And I'd become a vengeful god and live up in
the sky."

"But now you must stay on the ground," Hath-
gar did proclaim,
"And live along with mortal men, I know it is a
shame.
For you were made to be a god, the beard gave
you the right.

41

But Thor, the god of Thunder, stole it in the
night.
From you he took the power, to reign up in the
sky
You surely must be devastated, the fight was
just a lie."

"I gave Thor the power?" Swensen asked and
scratched his head.
"I thought you said that if we fought, I'd surely
leave him dead."
"A wicked trick he played upon you, I know it
was not right.
He sliced your beard and took it, and didn't
have to fight.
And when you hear the thunder from the heav-
ens in the sky,
It's Thor now telling all who hear, that next
time you will die."

From that day forth when storms occur, along
the Viking coast,
Swensen gathers all the warriors around, to
hear his might boast,
How the loud and ringing thunder, that fills
their very ears,
Is really Thor proclaiming, about his greatest
fears.

DONALD FREDERICKSON

That Swensen's beard is growing, and again be
long once more.
Then he will rise up to the sky, to fight the great
god Thor.

The Ritual

The mist rose slowly from the cold dark fiord,
As the glow of dawn crept over the sight.
Smooth was the water lapping the shore;
Calm was the air, as day birthed from night.
The frost upon the ground, the sign of a cold
morn.
Shown with a sparkle, by early morn light.

The bucket she carried was old and scarred.
Its water drawn from a cold dark pool.
Filled at a pool by the base of the cliff,
Fallen from above and cupped like a jewel,
Collected each day at first morning light
For a ritual cleansing--an act of renewal.

Placed by the door of the little stone house
It awaited the master--the start of his day.
He'd splash his face and dunk his head,
and wash in the Viking way,
To flush the vile spirits caught during the night,

DONALD FREDERICKSON

Hiding within him and wanting to stay.
The man gazed down at his eager young son.
T'was time to learn a man's way of life.
Braced for the cold, he uttered an oath,
Over the water brought by his wife.
And, into the bucket he plunged his head,
The ritual that daily cleansed his life.

The little boy watched water stream down his
face,
And winced at the thought of the cold.
The rituals of Vikings now his to learn,
He strived to stand tall and bold.
The time had now come to take his place.
Today he turned five years old.

The shock bit hard as his head went down;
The liquid filled his ears and nose.
The water held him in its ice-cold grip.
The pain flowed from his head to his toes.
He held his breath and his face felt numb--
But, he smiled as he arose.

His father nodded as he watched the boy.
In his heart was a strong, warm glow.
A Viking must never show pain nor fear,
A blemish for all to know.
His son would become a man one day,
And his courage would always show.

The Dance of the Maidens

She dances in circles so light on her feet
Around the tall pole, to music that's sweet.
With joy in her heart that winter's now past,
The first rites of spring have now come at last.
Around the May pole the young maidens twirl
Holding the ribbons, raised high as they swirl.

A wreath of new flowers rests o're her brow,
A sign the new season, again has come now.
Picked in the woods at morning's first light,
When first they did open, at the end of the
night.
Woven with care, this band of fresh flowers,
bestows upon her, new feminine powers.

Golden blond hair and sparkling blue eyes,
With a radiant smile upon which she relies
To catch the attention of a virile young man,
A potential suitor who will seek her hand,
Letting him know her new stage in life,
That she's now of an age, to become a wife.

DONALD FREDERICKSON

She's a young maiden, no longer a girl,
To the beat of the music she continues to twirl.
Around the May Pole with abandon she'll
dance,
With joy in her heart, and hope for romance.
She whirls and she twirls around and about,
And to the young men, she tries to stand out.

He stands, as he watches the young madens
dance,
Those darling young women who look for ro-
mance.
He spots the young woman; his heart does now
soar.
Struck with her beauty, he's intrigued to know
more.
His eyes gaze upon her, his smile put in play.
Coyly she glances, and then looks away.

Dancing now for him, she will let it show,
He is the one that she wants to know.
Light is her heart, as it starts to soar.
This dashing young man is now at the core
Of womanly yearning to have and to hold;
A daring young man, who's handsome and bold.

She whirls and she twirls, to her heart's delight
Secure in the knowledge she'll meet him this
night.

TALES OF THE VIKINGS

The "Dance of the Maidens" a tradition in
spring,
Around the May pole, to which the bards sing,
Is for the young women, who have come of age,
Recognized by the tribe, to embrace life's new
stage.

The drums have stopped beating, the dancing is
done.
She catches his eye and then starts to run.
Into the woods and down the faint trail,
Like a sprite of the forest, she seems to sail.
Enchanting, enticing, with him she does play.
And now on her trail, he'll continue to stay.

On through the forest is a glen by a stream,
babbling and bubbling, the place of her dream
To meet the young man who has caught her
eye,
With hopes he's the one who'll make her heart
fly,
Soaring with joy as it leaps from her breast,
Filled with his love, and softly caressed.

Stopping to wait, she is a young maid
Following the ritual, the way game's played.
Luring the young man into the wood,
To a place of romance, it is understood.

DONALD FREDERICKSON

Young hearts will seek each other to hold
When given the chance, in this ritual so old.

With the fresh flowers that bloom in the spring,
The dance of the maidens is considered to bring
Young hearts together to spark into flame,
And grow with a passion they'd not want tame.
To fine one another in this ritual in May,
Is the way of the Vikings, on this special day.

The Drakkar
(English Translation: Dragon Ship)

The prow of the dragon holds its head high,
The mark of a predator that's made out of pine.
Carved by a master with long graceful strokes,
Intricately cut, interwoven and fine.
The spirit of Oden, a sign of his wrath;
An object to fear is this Viking sign.

Forward it peers, through waves high and low,
Scaring vile spirits that prey the dark seas.
A beast with the courage to face the great
storms
And fight through victorious, and find a strong
breeze.
It hosts the brave warriors that cling to its back
Who sail to far reaches, wherever they please.

Scales of bright colors, the skin of the beast,
Protect Oden's warriors where ever they sail.
Fifty round shields, all placed in a row
Fitted together and tied to each rail,

DONALD FREDERICKSON

Strung side by side the length of the deck
Traversing the vessel, its head to its tail.

The wings of the dragon are four dozen ores,
To be used when the wind is light,
Pulled from the hull in rhythmic strokes
Cupping the water with every bite,
Drawn by men's hands, callused and strong
Pulled over, and over, with all of their might.

The spirit of Oden, great god of the north,
T'is the soul of each vessel; his wrath it does
show.
A hundred brave men, on the dragon's back
ride,
To dark deeds and plunder they go.
The beast of the Vikings will take them south,
In the direction the spring winds blow.

They set a square sail to catch Oden's breath,
For it's time to set the beast free.
To run with the wind and brave strong waves
From the realm of the cold North Sea,
To the coasts of England and Scotland and
France,
Where the title "Barbarian" is theirs to be.

The beast of the Vikings, Oden's gift to his race,
Carried bold warriors to many a land.

TALES OF THE VIKINGS

For more than three centuries they sailed the
dark seas
On the back of a dragon, steered deftly by man.
They plundered and pillaged and colonized too.
Into history they sailed and forever will stand.

DONALD FREDERICKSON

The Execution

Withering white whips of mist slowly rise
Above the cold water, and reach for the skies.
Over the ridge comes the first light of morn,
Caressing the fiord, as a new day is born.
Pulling the spirits of the day from the night,
No longer hiding, they enter the light.

The spirits renewal, with the birth of each day,
Give strength to a man, the Vikings would say;
To greet each new day, a gift from the gods,
In the light of the morn, and against many odds,
To call out to Oden, great god in the sky,
And loudly profess, "It's a good day to die."

His oath now proclaimed, a man would stand
fast
Accepting the fate, for him the gods cast,
To live life with honor or die like a man.
 The code of a Viking, on which he did stand,
Was given by Oden, the rules for his best,
And often a man was put to the test.

TALES OF THE VIKINGS

The spirits were silent, as the man slowly rose,
An omen of death, to quench his life flows.
A man of great courage, one few men would
face,
Among Oden's warriors, he held a high place.
His honor was questioned; three men were now
dead.
His skill as a warrior t'was lethal they said.

The chief of the clan, upon council relied,
Determined the laws of the land be applied.
The killing of men, in war was allowed,
And duels to the death formally avowed.
But fights in a mead hall, when drink was the
cause,
Disrupted society, of men bound by the laws.

The rules of the clan, on simplicity were based;
A life for a life was the verdict he faced.
Satisfaction demanded the families of three
To be given this morning, for the whole clan to
see.
At dawn's early light he knew he would face
An act of raw justice from the men of his race.

A man of strict honor, he'd come on his own
A feat of great courage, the clan would be
shown.

DONALD FREDERICKSON

No man constrained him, no bounds did he
wear;
His pride as a Viking was leading him there.
He entered the village with purposeful stride,
And the air of a warrior, in which he took pride.

To battle he'd go as he faced his last test,
and be granted a place, among Oden's best.
Only the Vikings who die in a fight,
Live life after death, a warrior's sole right.
T'is a gift of the gods, not granted to those
Who die in soft beds, snug in night clothes.

Calmly he stood, before those who judged him,
Accepting his fate; one that was grim.
They gave him his sword and shield for the
fight.
Armed as a warrior he now had the right
To die in a battle, but die by their hand,
A strict act of justice, in this frozen land.

Poised as a warrior and ready to die,
He looked his opponent straight in the eye.
Sword held to the front and shield to the side ;
Prepared for a fight, on this stance he relied.
Each time in battle might be a man's last.
If death is to come, they hope it is fast.

He gripped his sword tight and held the point
high,
And screamed with a roar, his great battle cry.
The executioner stood tall and pulled his sword
back,
For now was the time to start his attack.
The ark of the blade, ran true it did show,
Killing the warrior with one fateful blow.

Dying in battle was a fate that was best,
And with solemn reverence, they laid him to
rest.
Upon his stout boat was a great funeral pyre,
Twas cast out to sea and then set afire.
His soul flew to Oden, now one of his clan;
An honorable death was given this man.

DONALD FREDERICKSON

The Viking Maiden

There sits a young maiden with long golden
hair,
Shinning blue eyes, and skin that is fair.
Awaiting her true love to come into sight;
To kiss her again, and hold her so tight.
Within his strong arms, there'd be no more fear.
She needed him close, once more to be near.

Westward she watches the bright golden sun
Nearing the water, its days work now done.
And seeks the square sail, if only a trace,
A silhouette dark, on the water's gold face,
The return of the longboat that left on a quest
Taking her lover on his warrior's first test.

He sailed on a longboat for England's north
shore,
To find fortune and fame, and worlds to ex-
plore.
To fight with the raiders would make him a
man;
A Viking of stature, he said was the plan.

And when he returned, a bride she would be,
To a warrior of Oden, for the whole clan to see.

§

The fighting was fierce, this time when they
came.
The Celts were their waiting to kill and to maim.
Fear quenched by hatred did cause them to
fight,
As warriors of darkness who attacked in the
night.
Surprising those Vikings they found fast asleep,
They killed with a vengeance; their hatred was
deep.

Many war-boats returned from their quest,
The warriors of Oden had faced a hard test.
Booty they brought, but warriors they left,
The cost to the clan, for their annual theft.
Many had sailed to far distant lands.
Not all returned, as had been their plans.

The days were now shorter, the cold setting in,
He should have been back, too long it has been.
She lived day-by-day as pain pierced her breast,
With increasing fear, she tearfully confessed.
She petitioned to the gods and made a strong
plea,
For him to return with the men from the sea.

DONALD FREDERICKSON

Down to the shore she comes night-after-night,
Watching and waiting to catch the first sight
Of a sail in the distance, by the suns fading rays,
and a boat coming home to bring joy to her
days,
And with it her lover, her reason for life.
She'd wed him and bed him and be his sweet
wife.

§

The sun touched the surface and turned a
bright red,
An omen for her, before the day fled.
The soul of her warrior now lit up the skies,
And with its brief passing, she saw his demise.
His face she could see in the bright shining light,
And view now with anguish, their terrible
plight.

"Weep not, my love," the face seemed to say.
"The gods may be fickle, but we'll have our way.
One day you'll join me and here I will wait,
Again we'll be lovers; I know it's out fate."
Pain filled her breast and grew more intense,
scorched by the fire of ended suspense.

She watched the sun sink, down into the sea,
Gone, he was now, she knew it to be.

Killed as a warrior, it marked him a man.
It brought a great honor to him and the
clan.
He'd live on with Oden, great god in the sky,
The gift to a man, who in battle did die.

§

Her heart now was empty; she longingly cried
For the love of the man, who had left her and
died.
Not quite a widow, but betrothed when he
died,
She turned to clan on which she relied.
Grieve as a widow, they allowed her to mourn
As the wife of the warrior, without any scorn.

Her face rubbed with ashes to show the tear
streaks.
For a length of two moons, to no one she
speaks,
And stays by herself from morning to night,
To let them all know of her anguish and plight.
Lost in her pain, her heart tries to mend.
She has to go on, at least to pretend.

§

With mourning behind her, she must embrace
life.
Within the clan now, she's considered a wife,

DONALD FREDERICKSON

Whose man went to sea and never came back,
Giving her status that most women lack.
She now has the right to hold her head high
As wed to a warrior, who in battle did die.

Vikings killed fighting were granted their place
With a life after death, that other's can't face.
His honor now hers, the tribe realized,
Was carried with pride, which they recognized.
One day she'd leave the world they were in,
And in the next life, would again be with him.

THE OLD MAN

Up in the woods, cold creeps though the trees,
Bringing the harshest of winter's deep freeze.
Ice coated pines with bright shinny snow,
Snap with the thunder of Oden's great bow.
Silence then reigns for listening ears,
In the cold icy world that heightens man's fears.

A land of harsh winters that challenge the soul
Freezing and killing and taking their toll,
On those who defy them and live in this land,
Building their homes and taking a stand.
They face bitter cold, and each winter's ice,
With wood from the summer, on which they
suffice.

Each house a fortress to keep out the cold,
built solid with timber and sod that is rolled.
On roofs and the sides, they lay it on thick
To block winter spirits, that'll find a hole quick,
And hold in the warmth a fire will bring,
With a great pile of wood, to last until Spring.

DONALD FREDERICKSON

§

Deep in the valley, far from the town,
Is a small cottage that's old and run down.
Weathered and worn it needs proper care,
Or face the fierce winter with sides that are
bare.
It stands by a stream coated with ice.
A tired old house, it has to suffice.

The home of the trapper, a man bent and old,
Is drabby and drafty, and most often cold.
Too old to fix it and too old to care,
Time is now close, for life to end there
Away from the clansmen who live in the town.
Old and decrepit, they both are run down.

A fierce Viking warrior, in youth he was known,
But long are the years since reverence was
shown.
Old and forgotten they knew not his feats
Of battles hard fought, and with no retreats.
T'is the heart of a warrior in the shell of a man,
A life lived this long, had not been his plan.

Now thin and frail, a man of great years,
One still around, who out lived his peers.
Wars had left wounds that did not quite heal,
Leaving him pain which daily he'd feel.

He never complained and not let it show,
But walked with a shuffle, hunched over low.

§

Nights when the cold sweeps down from the
north,
Demons of ice gods, then will come fourth.
 Spirits of winter flirt in the moon's light,
Clinging and clutching throughout the night.
Dancing in shadows they hide while they seek
Something to torment--something that's weak.

The howl of the wolves, rings through the trees,
Petitioning the spirits, as their source of food
flees,
Leaving them hungry with little to eat;
Forming a pack they seek larger meat.
A deer they will pull down, a bear they will
fight,
A man they'll attack in the dark of the night.

The spirits of ice make strong victims weak,
Food for the wolves, the substance they seek.
On the coldest of nights, they howl a great cry,
Calling the spirits on which they rely,
To provide them a victim, one they'll take down,
That has enough meat to go all around.

DONALD FREDERICKSON

§

Within the small house, the old man's all alone.
Tending his hearth, he's chilled to the bone.
The spirits of cold, seep through the cracks,
Seeking their victim with icy attacks.
Ever relentless they grab and they hold
In the icy embrace of their deadly cold.

Gone is his woodpile; there should have been
more,
Put up in summer--a long winter's store.
He'd split what he could for the cold winter
nights.
But tired he was, and the wounds from the
fights
Ached with a vengeance from years now long
past.
He'd done what he could, but what he had
didn't last.

The fire is dwindling; its flame won't last long.
And with dying embers, he hears the wolf's
song.
Without a warm fire, the sign man's strength,
They will come seeking, and go to great length
To tear at the windows and chew at the doors.
To get in the house they'll dig under the floors.

TALES OF THE VIKINGS

He has not the heart to lay down and die
Succumbing to cold without even a try,
But to leave the world fighting, if only once
more
As a warrior of Oden; it's what he strives for.
Great gods of the North, see the man's plight,
And granting a gift, they give him a fight.

Donning old armor, now tarnished and stained,
Along with his helmet tis all that remains
Of days as a warrior from a time now long past,
To be used in this battle, which will be his last.
Dressed as a warrior he tries to stand straight,
To make the gods proud, he'd accepted his fate.

Wolves will be waiting, outside of the door.
Mean vicious killers, its him they came for.
He'll die in a battle; A smile crosses his face
Realizing that soon he'd take his place,
And enter the realm of Oden's great clan
of warriors killed fighting, while taking a stand.

The sign they are waiting rings through the
night,
The howl of the wolves from the pack he will
fight.
Killers who'd circle and come from each side,
Charging and slashing, a fight they'd provide.

DONALD FREDERICKSON

Ready for battle, his ax in one hand;
With sword in his other, he'll now take his
stand.

Out through the door and into the night,
And with a great roar, he is ready to fight.
The pride of a warrior sweeps over him,
Providing a strength that age cannot dim.
He stands in defiance, the gods can well see,
And old Viking warrior-- a right his to be.

Cold are the eyes of the head of the pack,
Dark shinning embers, to lead the attack.
The strongest and meanest, of those it did lead;
Vicious when challenged, it made others bleed.
Consumed with a hatred for all of mankind,
Snarls in anger at the sight of this find.

Rage filled its being, a need to fulfill,
Standing before him is a man it could kill.
Others it hunted, on dark lonely nights,
Killing them quickly without any fights.
Terror it brought to the community,
A man killing wolf, that's still running free.

Old and defiant, with weapons in hand,
To fend each attack, was his battle plan.

TALES OF THE VIKINGS

He knew they would start, a wolf at a time,
From bottom to top of their order, they'd climb.
And when he was weak, the fight almost done,
The leader would kill, to show it had won.

§

One crept from the left, and a flash from the
right,
Two wolves upon him, it started the fight.
Hard swung the ax with its two sided blade,
Seeking it's victim is how the fights played.
And lying before him are two fallen foes,
Fast lethal work from the weapon he chose.

Defiant he stands and glares at the pack.
The dead at his feet would soon be a stack.
Standing up straight, he looks to the sky,
Arms stretched above, and weapons held high.
"Oden," he yells, "you gave me this fight
Again I'm a warrior, I still claim the right."

Faster they come from the right and the left,
Biting and slashing, their movements are deft.
Wounds he is taking, but wounds he deals out,
The dead at his feet are scattered about,
Dealt by a warrior with weapons of old,
Cutting and slashing, the Viking is bold.

DONALD FREDERICKSON

The ice coated ground is covered in red,
Attests to the wounds from which it was fed.
His arms now are weary, his breath hard to
catch.
Still are were coming; his life they will fetch.
He wheels in a circle to keep them at bay,
Weapons held forward, a threat they relay.

He stands in defiance; at the head wolf he
glares,
An opponent of merit, which had been his
prayers.
Soon he would meet the lethal attack;
The one to be dealt by the head of the pack.
A lobo of merit, the killer of men,
Will enter this fight and bring on the end.

Suddenly it charges, to impose its will,
And go for the throat to make a fast kill .
It sprang through the air with a vicious attack.
The force of the blow put the man on his back.
Weapons lay scattered, no more could be used.
Laying defenseless, he lay there confused.

Over his body the wolf stands in place,
The drool from its mouth falls onto his face.
And with a loud snarl, it lays its teeth bare,
Biting deep in the neck, to end this affair.

TALES OF THE VIKINGS

Raising its head, it howls into the night
Telling the world that it won the fight.

Oden looked down from his place in the sky.
And with a broad smile, he watched the man
die.
Old may he be, his heart in the mode,
He went into battle with his Viking code.
And died as a warrior, who now had the right
To live with the gods, well pleased in their sight.

DONALD FREDERICKSON

The Storm

Out of the fiord, it sails in dawn's light
A drakkar of war, to show the world fright.
Both ends are pointed, its head and its tail,
With a mast in the center to hold the square sail.
Thirty stout ores, half to each side,
cup the cold water on the outgoing tide.

On a raised prow, a dragon's head stands,
Protection while sailing to far distant lands.
Bright glowing eyes peer o're the dark seas,
Watching for danger, within the stout breeze,
Waiting for spirits from deep in the sea,
To scare them away and scowl as they flee.

Spirits and demons from far down below,
Prey upon those who dare to go
Across the great sea to a far distant shore,
Transgressing their realm, an act they deplore.
Theirs is the water, deep, dark and cold,
Jealously guarded from sailors so bold.

TALES OF THE VIKINGS

The sun rises slowly, as they sail from the north,
Away from the fiord from which they came
forth
To find a fair wind to sail them ahead
Over the sea that fills men with dread.
Safe on the back of their beast made for war,
They sail the vast sea, toward a far away shore.

For a day and a night there is a stiff breeze
To set a fair sail, that pulled them with ease.
Across the great sea, so solemn and deep,
Sailed the fierce dragon, that was in their keep.
It took the tall waves and rode them with pride,
This beast of the Vikings on which they did ride.

Great gods of the seas, looked up from below; a
calm easy passage they would not bestow.
They called on the lighting and thunder so loud,
And made choppy seas, within a dark cloud.
And, summoned sea spirits, to join them and
fight
The ship of the Vikings, in the dark of the night.

A wave rose above, and over them hung,
With the face of a serpent, complete with
forked tongue.
The dragon stood tall and took it on straight,
Sliced it in two and then looked to its mate.

DONALD FREDERICKSON

A wave twice the size of the one it just faced
Washed over the dragon, and then away raced.

Bright streaks of lightning tearing the air
Followed by thunder--the mighty pair.
Down came the mast, split and on fire,
Tangled in ropes, their future looked dire.
Rain lashed them harshly, driven by wind.
On the deck of the Drakkar, the men were now
pined.

The boat of the Vikings, a dragon at heart,
Met the sea monster, and fought from the start.
Raging in anger, faced charge after charge,
The waives of the demon that were oh so large.
Battered and broken, it still held its own,
In a fight to the death, in this sea all alone.

Fury met courage as the battle ran forth,
Both mighty forces in this sea in the north.
The demon lashed out with all of its might,
To sink the wild dragon, with which it did fight.
Wind, waves and lightning it threw at its foe,
Sent with the fury of the sea gods below.

Eyes glowing like embers, its nostrils did smoke,
Facing fierce charges, it never once broke.

TALES OF THE VIKINGS

Defiant it battled-- refused to back down,
The will of the Vikings, known as renown,
T'is soul of a vessel unwilling to break,
riding the sea within the storm's wake.

The fury abated as the beast spent its rage.
The dragon the victor, in the final stage,
Sat there defiant both battered and torn,
A smile on its face, one proud to be worn.
The sea sent its worst to give it a fight,
And ran away fleeing when facing its might.

DONALD FREDERICKSON

The Trapper's Dogs

Deep in the woods cold creeps through the
trees,
Relentlessly probing within the deep freeze,
Over the snow, with its blanket of white,
Along icy streams, frozen solid and tight.
Down from the north, with stealth it does slip,
Grasping the world in its icy cold grip.

The face of the moon shines in the night,
Ringed with a haze of a soft filtered light,
Outlining the trees, the snow covered pines,
That sparkle and twinkle in intricate lines.
The woods come alive with subtle contrast,
A scene of great beauty, until the moon's past.

A small glowing fire shines cheery and warm,
Flickering bright light in its natural form,
Highlighting the camp within the tall trees,
A beacon of life from which the cold flees.
It's warmth for the trapper, along with his dogs,
When fed through the night, with additional
logs.

TALES OF THE VIKINGS

A good day of trapping provided the pelts
Stretched out and drying, on racks of stout belts
To be sold in the markets of far distant towns,
By Viking traders, on which the world frowns.
Be they merchants or raiders, whichever they
choose,
When sailing their Drakkars, upon a long cruise.

In front of the fire, the trapper does sit
Smoking his pipe, while keeping it lit;
Watching the embers that come from the
flames.
Recounting his youth, to which he still claims
Was filled with the honor of battles well fought;
Confronting an enemy was all that he sought.

Now old and tired he sits by the flame,
Gone are the days when men knew his name.
Only the young, those made in his mold,
Follow the tradition of those that are bold,
Making the voyages that fill men with dread;
The raids of the Vikings like he had once lead.

Flames from the fire fight the cold of the night.
Hot glowing rays that show its great might,
Bring warmth to the trapper and his two dogs,
Who bask in its heat, as he feeds it logs.

DONALD FREDERICKSON

Nodding and napping within its safe keep,
The old Viking trapper was falling asleep.

Out of the darkness, howls pierce the cold
night,
A sign that the wolves are ready to fight.
Driven by hunger they form in a pack,
Looking for prey which they can attack.
Dangerous and deadly, they'll take on a man.
He's now only food, meat for their clan.

Clutching his ax, a blade from the past,
The trapper knows well he'll have to stand fast,
In the light of the fire, the flames the beasts
fear;
T's the circle of combat, when soon they come
near.
One on each side, his dogs with him stand,
Teeth bared and growling, to face the wolf
band.

Obtained from a litter of dogs bred for war,
A mean vicious nature, the breed is known for.
Raised from small puppies, they seem rather
mild,
were trained by the man to fight wolves in the
wild.

TALES OF THE VIKINGS

The old man's companions were known as his
pets,
But fighters they be, where one could place
bets.

Two embers of gold shown deep from the trees
pinpoints of danger from which all life flees.
Dark eyes of the leader, reflecting the flames
Back to the trapper and his dogs with no
names.
Moving in boldly, wolves enter the light,
Snarling and growling and ready to fight.

Both dogs move forward, taking their place,
Standing together where they can now face
The first of the wolves that'll come charging in.
They'd protect the old man from the following
din,
Providing the line of the trappers defense,
Stopping the wolves without any pretence.

Standing there waiting with ax in his hand,
The man and his dogs face the wolf band.
Ready they are, to meet the wild pack
And kill one or two before sending them back
Into the woods, in the dark of the night,
Running in fear from the dogs trained to fight.

DONALD FREDERICKSON

Facing these dogs, bread large and for war
Was something the wolves had done twice
before.
The last confrontation cost half of their pack.
Only their hunger had made them come back.
Now facing the carnage the war dogs could
make,
Drove fear deep within them, making them
quake.

Standing there shaking they sensed twas not
smart
to boldly come forward; they had not the heart.
With pain in their bellies and fear in their eyes,
A primal instinct foretold their demise.
Backing off slowly, both hungry and cold,
The price to be paid for not being bold.

The man watched them go with a smile on his
face.
In the depth of these woods, they still knew his
place.
And back to the fire, the dogs and man went
To light up his pipe and puff quite content.
And doze in the warmth, held within its em-
brace
Without a care in the world, not even a trace.

THE TALISMAN

Deep in the forest is a spiritual place
Reserved for the gods, the superior race.
A place of great beauty when seen in the night
During a full moon, portrayed in its light;
The great hall of Odin, framed by moon rays
Filtered through trees, the way the light plays.

The spirit of Odin and those of his race,
Dwell in the garden of this spiritual place,
Framed by the moon in its radiant glow
Transforming the heavens, to the earth below;
Bringing the gods to come from on high,
And hear her petition, a heartfelt cry.

Upon the north wind, in the light of the moon
Traverses the mournful wail of a Lune
Cutting the silence in the deep of the night,
Foretelling the awakening of dawn's early light,
Announcing their presence in this holy place
The gods from above, whom she will face.

DONALD FREDERICKSON

Ritually bathed and dressed in all white;
Preparations she made, for this special night.
T'is the young maid, on a spiritual quest
To beseech the gods and make a request,
To give her a tallasman for her lover to wear,
To keep him from harm, is her devout prayer.

Alone in the forest, she wanders at length,
Seeking the spirit with Odin's great strength,
To be given to man within the moon's light
When its face is full, at the end of the night.
To her, who will seek it, and show reverence
While petitioning the god, for his assistance.

 Her quest is a pool, deep dark and cold,
Ancient and sacred, and invariably old.
Protected by spirits, before morning's light,
Who flee from the moon at the end of the
night.
Its waters are magic, to which it is known
Have a great power, it has been shown.

A gift from the gods, the water of life
Springs from a rock, seared by Thor's knife.
Not a flow but a trickle, which clings to the wall
From a cliff in the forest, from which it does fall.

TALES OF THE VIKINGS

It seeps through the moss, moist green and stiff,
To rest in the pool at the base of the cliff.

The drip of the water makes its own tune.
Drop after drop, in the face of the moon,
Gaining great strength, within the soft glow.
T'is sought by the maiden; its powers bestow,
When captured in ritual, on a special night
Will protect her fair love, in the coming fight.

Lighted by moonbeams, to show her the way,
The trail through the forest, so she will not
stray.
She follows the loon, its call in the night
Guiding her along on the path that is right.
In her quest to petition the gods on this night,
She'll perform sacred rituals, well pleased in
their sight.

Entering the cathedral of living trees,
The place of the gods, to which she now sees.
Bathed in the moonlight, t'is a sight to behold,
Radiant in splendor, for the deities of old.
Its alter, the pool, the rays do highlight,
Finding it now, her quest is in sight.

DONALD FREDERICKSON

In a ritual of reverence, she kneels by the pool
Peering deep in the water, so pure and so cool.
Beholding the power of Odin on high;
Beseeching his mercy, she'd come to rely,
Upon the old gods, to relieve her alarm
To protect her true love, and keep him from
harm.

She mouths ancient chants, meant only for gods
Imploring their help, against any odds.
To use their great power, to guide and protect
The love of her life, so she can expect
He'll return from the voyage o're the dark sea.
And again his strong arms, around her will be.

She dips a glass vile, the size of a ring
Into the water of the sacred spring.
Scooping a drop, or perhaps maybe two,
Then sealing the top with a cork colored blue.
She looks to the heavens, to mouth a short
prayer,
Then quickly, with reverence, departs from
there.

Attached to the vile is a cord made of leather
Clutching the talisman, a strong sturdy tether.

Around her love's neck, she'll place it with care.
For Odin' protection, will now be there.
To wear into battle, or sail the dark sea;
To return to her safely, she knows it will be.

DONALD FREDERICKSON

Homecoming

They cut the water once, they cut the water
twice.
In cadence to their rhythmic pace, they cut the
water thrice.
Slowly forward crept the beast, the captain at
the prow,
The war ship of the Vikings, the one that would
endow
Their legacy for years to come, the one the
world would know,
Spread o're the seas upon its back wherever
they would go.

Upon the seas they'd sailed afar, to ply thier
fatal trade,
Along the coast of England to make raid after
raid.
They filled their ship with plunder, as much as it
would hold,
The spoils of war within thier grasp, much silver
and much gold.

The raiding and fighting done, t'was time to
turn about,
Returning to their homeland now, with riches
they would flout.

The dragon's head upon the prow, the one the
world did dread.
Sought the entrance to thier home, upon the
shore ahead.
In cadence to the drum's soft beat they firmly
set their oars,
And slowly pulled the boat along, between the
fiord's shores.
And to the lyre from which it birthed, the beast
returned today,
And brought the Viking raiders home, within
this month of May.

The women of the hamlet, stood on the sandy
shore
As joy swelled up within their breasts to see the
ship once more.
For once again the warriors came, returning
from the sea,
To hold them close in their strong arms, as it
was meant to be.
The fear they held for those who'd left upon
their dangerous quest,

DONALD FREDERICKSON

Now quenched with joy and set aside; they
once again were blest.

Upon the prow, the captain stood and called
out to the town.
"We're home again, victorious now, as warriors
we're renown.
We're back today from our long quest, across
the cold dark sea.
We're home again in our fiord, a place we're
meant to be.
We have with us much bounty, from the life we
chose to live,
And to the women of our tribe, we've many
gifts to give."

The procession held a cheerful air, as each man
left the boat,
Arms laden full of precious goods, as much as
he could tote,
To carry to his family, his children and his wife,
The spoils of war that he had gained, a tribute
to his life.
To each he brought a wealth of gifts, that he
had won with pride,
To see a smile on his child's face, and one upon
his bride.

There'd be a celebration, t'wd last most of the
night
To commemorate the warriors, who sailed away
to fight.
A feast they'd have for everyone, they'd come
from miles around,
And celebrate with those returned , and now
were safe and sound.
Within the dark foreboding fiord, which cupped
them in the night,
Would come the sounds of merriment in a shin-
ning speck of light.

They set an ox to roasting, so each could have
his fill
of all the food one could consume, whatever
that he will.
Large bowls there were with vegetables, over-
flowing at the rim,
Along with jugs of sweet liquor, filled right up to
the brim.
A place there was for everyone, each member
of the clan
to celebrate the homecoming of each seafaring
man.

And when the meal was ended, and all con-
sumed their fill,

DONALD FREDERICKSON

Would come the stories of brave raids, and
blood that they did spill.
They'd sing of sailing savage seas and facing
raging storms,
As vengeful gods from far below blew hard on
mighty horns
That brought the thunder and the rain and jag-
ged bolts of light,
To test the strength of their war ship, through-
out the darkest night.

With the speeches left behind, the instruments
would play,
And rough and ready warriors would dance the
night away.
Their steps were light and lively, within the fire
light.
Upon this eve of homecoming, there'd be no
need to fight.
For twas a celebration when the men again
came home,
And brought with them the booty from the world
that they did roam.

The Raid

"Vikings are coming, the Vikings are near"
Yelled the old priest consumed with cold fear.
He ran to the church to ring the loud bell
And tell the towns folk that all was not well.
The scourge of the north was now on it's way.
The worst of their fears would happen this day.

Three ships were sited o're the dark sea,
And would be upon them before they could
flee.
Vikings they were, they'd loot and they'd burn
Devastating the town was a major concern.
Face them they must, to stop them or die.
Again the priest yelled a hysterical cry.

"Look to the shore," the Viking did shout.
"See the far hamlet; turn this ship about.
A steeple I see which pokes through the trees
The sign of a town we'll sack as we please.

We'll take what we want and the gold that is there
Within the great church, and not say a prayer."

"A feast day it is, they sing and they dance
To honor their god who was pierced with a lance.
The tables are set with food in great store,
A meal for my warriors when we come ashore.
Again comes a day, to which I proclaim
Will add to the fear of our Viking name."

With a full sail they ran up to the shore .
And, from the village there came a loud roar
From the men of the clan who'd stand up and fight
These fierce northern warriors now coming in sight.
They lined up against them, this horrible hoard
Of men from the north, who's raids they deplored.

Out of the ships men poured like dark ants
And formed on the beach in their battle stance.
They looked to the men that defended their town

TALES OF THE VIKINGS

With pitch forks and sickles they'd quickly go
down,
Felled by a sword or an ax's sharp blade.
To the warriors of Odin, t'is a game to be
played.

Each spring they came, raiding England's north
shore
To plunder the towns; t'is gold they looked for.
And silver and coins they'd add to their take
The spoils of a victory found in their wake,
To add to the wealth of Ragnar their king,
A Viking of stature to whom the bard's sing.

They charged up the shore with a fierce battle
cry,
To fight those who waited, and see who will die.
Cutting and slashing men died and were
maimed,
The victims of Vikings, which the world claimed
Were viscous warriors when engaged in a fight,
Wounding and Killing with all of their might.

Opposition behind them, they now faced the
town,
To sack and to loot and burn the place down.

DONALD FREDERICKSON

They entered the houses to steal what was
there,
To take what they would, without the least care.
Those who'd dared stop them were destined to
die.
Quickly they learned to not even try.

The towns folk all ran to get out of the way
Driven by fear on this fatal day.
Looking for safety where there was none;
Into the church they eventually would run.
Sanctuary was sought within the great hall
Away from the raiders who were killing them
all.

Inside they cowered, the doors they did lock.
Shaking with fear, they were the lord's flock.
Weeping and praying for help they all cried
Beseeching their God, upon whom they relied,
To protect them from harm on this fateful day;
"Deliver us safely," they continued to pray.

Ragnar the Viking, fierce warrior king,
Looked to the church and the wealth it would
bring.
Behind him the houses, flames now consumed,

which burned to foundations before he re-
sumed.
His assault on the church to bring it down,
Or set it on fire like the rest of the town.

"Pay me a tribute, it's what I demand
Or my men will destroy you, at my command.
A hundred pound weight in silver and gold
Then here I will leave, and again you'll be told
How the god you hold high has protected you.
But I'm here to tell you, it's simply not true."

"I am King Rangnar, Lord of the North,
He who decides who will come forth
To live or to die on this fated day,
Is only for me, and me only to say.
To those of his flock, I loudly proclaim
I want the old priest, whom I hold in distain."

A hundred weight gold and the priest I will take
Give them to me now, for your safety's sake.
Take only a moment to consider your fate,
For I'm not a man who's willing to wait.
But if church door, you'll not unlock
Then all will soon burn, the entire flock."

His wrath they could see, was against the old
priest.
If they gave him to them, they would be re-
leased
And shed of the Vikings that laid waste to their
land,
The men of the north from this raiding band.
The decision was simple, to live or to die
"The priest had to go," they said with a sigh.

From inside the rectory they slowly came out
with the wealth of church carried by the de-
vout.
A cache of bright gold soon lay at his feet,
Placed by the people who now knew defeat.
Shaking with fear they accepted their fate,
But in stone church, the old priest did await.

Dragged by two warriors, one on each side,
The priest came unwilling and all the time cried.
Tied to a tree with his feet in the air
An inverted cross, to enhance his despair.
Five men with bows let stout arrows fly
Into the priest and all watched him die.

"I am the victor; my god will reign here,"
Ragnar proclaimed on those that did fear.

"T'is Odin who guides us, great god of the north
And we are the warriors who he has brought
forth
To sail the world over which are in his plans
To raid and to conquer in far away lands."

They sailed with boats laden, as Ragnar looked
back
At the smoke rising slowly, left from their at-
tack.
Wealth he'd acquired, both fortune and fame
And once again, spread the fear of his name .
They were the Vikings with fierce Nordic pride
Warriors of Odin, on whom they relied.

The Berserker

The wind blew strongly from the North to fill
the single sail.
With Odin's breath to push it, their mission
would not fail.
First boat in an armada, a hundred more there
be,
Heading to the English coast, across the cold
dark sea.
All sailing to the South this spring, to wage
another war;
They'd fight the Celts who waited there, upon
the barren shore.

Beside the dragon prow he stood. They both
peered out to sea
To scan the far horizon, for whatever there may
be.
They sailed to make a landing. His boat was in
the lead,
A thousand men behind him, all held the war-
rior's creed.

To meet this day with honor, in battle with their
foes,
To kill or die while fighting, no matter how it
goes.

The enemy was sighted, another thousand
more,
Lined up in their formation, just beyond the
shore.
The Celts were of a single mind, that they
would win the fight,
And devastate the Viking hoard before this
coming night.
They spied the boats across the sea, all heading
for the shore
Filled with Viking warriors, the enemy they
deplore.

A hundred dragons lead the charge, across each
rolling wave
And on their backs the thousand rode, all war-
riors bold and brave.
Soon they'd make a landing, a fight there'd be
today,
For this they sailed the cold dark sea within this
month of May.
England was the grandest prize; It would be
theirs to take.

They'd route the Celtic army, laying devastation
in it's wake.

He shunned protective padding, the use of it
rejected.
 And from his neck down to his waist he would
not be protected.
Muscles taut across his back in wild anticipa-
tion;
The coming fight was soon to start; a cause for
jubilation.
In one hand he held an ax. In the other was a
sword,
The weapons weld by Viking men, to which the
world deplored.

"Odin give me strength today," he roared with
all his might,
"For many Celts I'll kill for you, within this com-
ing fight."
With booming voice and resonance, he cursed
the waiting foe
And called the spirits of the north, an icy breath
to blow
And cast a spell around to him, to give him
strength of ten
So he could kill the first he faced and then to
kill again.

Some men fight with vengeance, others with
cold skill;
A berserker trained for battle, will only fight to
kill.
He shuns the use of armor.   Weapons are his
just defense
When used in vicious on-slot, he only shows
offence.
T'is the bravest of the warriors, the strongest of
the clan,
A favorite picked by Odin, a superior fighting
man.

He screamed out vulgar curses to make his
temper grow,
And in a rage transformed himself and let the
anger flow.
His body shook and trembled; Anticipation in its
grip.
As blood lust rose within him, a drug that would
equip
The beserker as invincible, the champion of
gods above,
A warrior dealing savage death; the one that
they did love.

A thousand boats approached the shore; they
rode the inbound tide

And outpoured Viking warriors, who formed up
side by side.
Two armies, now their fate sealed. There would
be no recourse.
On one side were the Vikings, the Celts the op-
posing force.
The scent of fear drifts toward the horde, for
many men would die
Or be mauled by ax or blade, to make them
scream and cry.

Berserkers claim the first blows, an honor for
each man
As fiercest of the fighting men within the raid-
ing band.
They screamed their virulent curses, which fill
the sordid air
To tell the waiting foe, it's cause for their de-
spair.
Senses rose to breaking, the tension running
large
"T'is a good day to die," they scream; and then
they start to charge.

A thousand met a thousand, the warriors from
both sides,
To live or die in fierce combat is where their
fate resides

The berserker was to lead the charge and gain
his just reward
As first to kill awaiting Celts with mighty ax and
sword.
His weapons of destruction fell upon the wait-
ing foe,
Dispersing devastation, with every mighty blow.

Many Celts had faced him; most of them were
dead.
His savagery in battle, now filled their world
with dread.
Another death delivered, with each and every
blow
And warriors shied from facing him; their fear
began to show.
Retreating from his onslot, they pulled back
away from him,
And drew him in behind their line, through the
clamoring din.

A trap they laid to snare him, to stop this vi-
cious foe,
A savage young berseker who killed with every
blow.
Twenty men soon ringed him, their strategy
relied
Upon the force of numbers; they charged from
every side.

He whirled in a tight circle and met them blow
for blow,
And slashed and killed with each onslot, and
still the blood did flow.

Odin viewed the battle, from his place up in the
sky,
And smiled at the young warrior, who looked
death in the eye.
He showed the courage of the code and fought
with all his might,
And never backed an inch away, from the fierc-
est of the fight.
Many Celts attacked him and many men were
dead.
The fighters sought to stop him and the blood
flowed fast and red.

The blood lust rose within him, to fill his soul
with rage,
And on the field of battle he held the center
stage .
A shield was shattered by his ax; his sword
pierced another chest
And on and on he fought with them, without
the need to rest.
The Celts kept him surrounded and charged
from every way,

For strength in numbers was the plan; it was
their power play.

For every man or two he killed, a wound af-
flicted him,
And drained his blood along with theirs, within
the battle's din.
His ax now moving slower, the sword thrust not
as straight,
His strength is flowing from him and he knew
his coming fate.
"I fought this fight with honor," he shouted to
the sky,
"And now it's time to leave this world; it is a my
day to die."

He stood with weapons poised, and no longer
could fight back
As Celtic swords stabbed from every side; it was
their last attack.
And there upon the battle field he expelled his
final breath.
A smile there was upon his face, he'd died a
warrior's death.
His soul would go to Assgard, it was his solemn
right
To live again among the gods, well pleased
within their sight.

Odin's Reward

Odin was a Viking god. He was their fieriest one
Who reigned in Valhala, far beyond the sun.
The God of War and Battles, fought with savage might,
He led the Viking warriors, however went the fight.
He gave them many victories, which brought Viking's fame,
And every time they went to war, they fought in Odin's name.

A warrior's code was followed, proclaiming how to die
And those who fell in battle found a place up in the sky.
An afterlife in Valhala, was claimed a warrior's right
When death was gained with honor, incurred within a fight.
And only Viking warriors would live again once more,
A special gift from Odin, the mighty God of War.

The "hall of fallen warriors", Valhala was the
place
For them to live eternally, the heroes of their
race.
Battle shields comprised the roof which rose
above the floors,
And all around the perimeter were five hundred
and forty doors.
Eight hundred men could enter, each door so
very wide
Together while in unison, and marching side by
side.

Each day they got a battle, again to live and
fight,
And every wound would heal, before the com-
ing night.
There was a banquet nightly, where Odin was
the host.
And battle hardened warriors would eat and
drink and boast.
It was the warriors just reward for bravery they
had shown,
While living up to Odin's code, the only one
they'd known.

Century upon century, they sailed in Odin's
name,

DONALD FREDERICKSON

Upon the cold north seas to spread their dread-
ed fame.
They raided and they plundered, and fought
with savage might.
The spoils of victory but a second roll, to how
they fought the fight.
And Odin watched from high above, a smile
upon his face,
The conquests of his warriors, as he ruled the
Viking race.

Thor

A resounding crash of thunder, announce the
coming war;
The battle of the giants, and the Viking god
named Thor.
Rolling clouds of darkness race from East to
West
Building with a great fury, to meet this deadly
test.
In his chariot pulled by goats, Thor rides across
this sky
And with it comes the thunder, rolling out as he
goes by.

He wields his mighty hammer, killing giants in
this fight,
As crashing bolts of lightning, throw fingers of
bright light.
A mighty battle rages forth, within the storm
this night.

And in his wake the carnage lay, resulting from
the fight.
Again the mighty warrior god has stopped their
enemy,
To save the world of gods above, and keep it's
harmony.

A long red beard upon his face; he stares
through blazing eyes,
And when compared to other gods, is huge in
body size.
Three weapons does he carry, which are well
known at length,
His hammer held with iron gloves, and a belt
that gives him strength.
He is the strongest of the gods, of trolls and gi-
ants too,
And with each and every one he kills, his
strength he does renew.

The mightiest of warriors, he defeats foe after
foe
Be they be Giant, troll or sea serpent, off to
their death they go.
He is Protector of the Gods, in Asgard where
they roam
And quells attacks of those giants, who would
destroy their home.

And in the land of mortal men, there's no rea-
son for alarm,
For with his warrior's skills, it too is free from
harm.

Worshiped by the Viking men, he was their god
of war,
For warriors living now, and those who lived
before.
The embodiment of bravery, and courage in a
fight
Thor was the noble god, who stood out in the
light
He was a Viking hero; his warrior's code held
dear.
His followers, known around the world, were
men who knew no fear.

DONALD FREDERICKSON

King Ragnar's Revenge

The dragon's head above the bow, led them out
to sea,
And felt the spray upon its face, as cold as it
could be,
The sting of icy water; it splashed high o're the
rail.
A sign the sea's great strength, forever would
prevail,
Passage through the cold dark waves, in this
ocean of the north
Was but a gift, from gods below, as their great
boats sailed forth.

The snow had left their homeland; ice broke
upon the shore.
The cold dark sea, they now could sail, and go
on raids once more.
They left the northern fiords, and crossed the
frigid sea
On water filled with chunks of ice, as deadly as
could be.

The time was ripe for their revenge. These
Vikings of the north
Would avenge King Ragnar's death, and
southward they came forth.

A hundred ships all filled with men, and primed
to go to war.
Braved cold waves and cutting winds, to find
the distant shore.
Upon their beasts of burden, they sailed both
day and night,
Five thousand Viking warriors, all looking for a
fight.
The heathen army from the north, was sailing
south this year
Led by Ragnar's wayward sons who held the
world in fear.

On to the coast of England, they sailed to the
southwest
To land an army on the shore, for their goal of
conquest.
Led by Seth the Boneless, a man who was intent
To have his final vengeance, a goal he'd not
relent.
He sought the king of England; t'was Ella who
wore the crown
He'd fight the noble's armies and they'd come
crashing down.

It was the death of Ragnar, when thrown in a
snake pit
That brought his sons together, to mend the
family split.
They were considered wayward, and sought to
steal his throne
Throughout the Viking kingdom, their animosity
was known.
Their father was a Viking king, and be that as it
may,
His sordid death within the pit, was not a
warrior's way.

All three sons vowed vengeance, they'd take on
England's king
And in the name of their father, retribution they
would bring.
And o're the icy waters, of the northern sea
They sailed to meet their fate; it was their
destiny.
On to the field of battle, they'd bring their
heathen force
And fight like savage beasts, these men known
as the Norse.

§

A fog outlined the coast, as dawn showed its
first light
And after days and nights at sea, land was a
welcome sight.
They set their course along the shore, to their

awaited fate
And sought the inland river ways, their boats
could navigate.
The Drakkars traversing on the streams, were a
sight to fear.
The symbol that the Viking horde, again was
coming near.

Upon a river they did chance, within the
morning light
And as they boldly entered it, their beasts
transformed to flight.
Against its flow their dragon's flew, pulled by
wooden wings,
In rhythm to the beating drums, to which the
cadence rings.
Slowly forward soared the beasts, now hunting
for their prey;
For it was time to make a kill, and start a war
today.

The presence of the long boats, strung out just
like a snake
One behind the other, kept close within its
wake.
A fearful beast the boats made, while trailing in
a line
And on its back five thousand rode; it was a
fatal sign

That soon would come the fighting, and many
men would die
At the hand of northern raiders, and their gods
up in the sky.

§

Church bells rang, to tell the town of danger on
its way.
Upon the river Vikings come, and they'd be
here today.
A wall there is around the town; defense it does
provide
When the gates are shut and barred, tightly
from inside.
All the people of the land, felt safe within their
town
And relied upon their king's forces, to cut the
heathens down.

Upon the field of battle, the king's army did
wait.
Again he'd fight the northern horde, and this
time seal their fate.
He'd send the Vikings packing, defeated by his
hand
Into the ships of war they brought, and back to
their homeland.
He'd stood up to the heathen horde, defeating
them before

Again he'd be the victor; it's what he had in
store.

The knights were primed and ready, with
shields and polished swords
To defend the English king, and reap their just
rewards.
The Vikings they awaited, since the sea had
shed its ice,
And trained hard for the coming fight, on which
they would suffice
Upon the skill they harbored, with the weapons
made for war.
And soon they'd put them to the test, as their
opponents came ashore.

Viking warriors poured from the boats and set
their battle stance
Into a pointed wedge they formed, from which
they would advance.
Five thousand met another five, and maybe a
bit more
As the mighty forces of two lands, fought upon
the river's shore.
Both sides were battle hardened, and fought
with all their might.
The give and take were much the same, from
early in the fight.
Sword met sword with vicious blows, all dealt
with great intent

DONALD FREDERICKSON

As scores of warriors fought and died, and yet
they'd not relent.
The blood flowed freely from their wounds, and
on the ground did lay,
A blanket colored crimson red, to mark the
fateful day.
Upon the ground the dead piled high, to mark
the fatal score.
And with the savage fighting, the toll rose more
and more.

Safely from the town's parapets, they watched
the battle rage
T'was history in the making, as it turned
another page.
They saw the Vikings savage push, and gain
upon the field
And when the tide had finally turned, their
future was reveled
King Ella's mighty army, defeated, broke and
ran.
And victory went to Ragnar's sons, conforming
to their plan.

A rope around King Ella's neck, now showed he
lost the fight,
They paraded him before the town, to show his
gruesome plight.
The wayward sons of Ragnar, would have their
just revenge

Dishonor of their father's death, was now theirs
to avenge
Into a viperous pit of snakes, Ragnar had been
cast
A death fit only for a slave, They'd right the
wrong at last.

A torture called "Blood Eagle", the death Ella
would receive
Excruciating in its pain, that nothing could
relieve
His ribs were cut along his spine and pulled
back to look like wings
and both lungs were filled with salt, to enhance
the pain it brings.
In shear terror Ella screamed, long and without
recourse
The sons of Ragnar watched him die and did
not feel remorse.

With the king of England gone, and his army
now in tatters,
Seth the boneless and brothers, addressed their
other matters.
They now were geared for more conquest, no
one was in their way.
Across the breath of England they went,
advancing day by day.
They took possession of the land and riches it
would bring,

DONALD FREDERICKSON

And the Seth, son of Ragnar, became the
English king.

Meet the Author

Donald W. Frederickson—Author

Mr. Frederickson is an exciting new author in the writing world. In the last three years he has published two new novels, written numerous short stories and gained some notoriety in local literary circles with his epic Viking poetry.

Mr. Frederickson has traveled extensively, providing experiences from which he draws liberally in his writing. He lived a year and a half in Eritrea, Africa during his military service, toured Europe with a backpack in the Sixties, and has taken many extensive trips into Mexico and Central America. His love for archaeology and the Maya civilization has led him to write "The Roar of the Jaguar", a historical fiction novel on one of the last great Maya warrior kings

Having retired ten years ago from an industrial executive position, Mr. Frederickson now spends his time traveling, writing and providing presentations on the Maya culture to libraries, museums and academic institutions.

www.ingramcontent.com/pod-product-compliance
Lightning Source LLC
Chambersburg PA
CBHW060520030426
42337CB00015B/1957